I0559825

THE SUGAR ATTACK

The Sugar Attack

Copyright © 2023 Trina Wiggins, M.D.

All rights reserved. No part of this book may be reproduced or transmitted in any form or by any means without written permission from the author.

Published by ELOHAI International Publishing & Media

P.O. Box 1883

Cypress, TX 77410

hello@elohaiintl.com

Illustrator: Husni Assaerozi

Scriptwriter: Gustavo Soria

Author Contact:

Dr. Trina Wiggins

trinawiggins.com

Opt2bfit.com

Dr. Trina Wiggins would like to recognize fellow Stanford Alumnus Phil Davis, who recommended she write a comic book for children about the harmful effects of sugar.

ISBN: 978-1-953535-75-7

CONTENTS

AND JUST LIKE THAT, THE INVADER, GALACTOSE, RELEASED THE BIGGEST THREAT TO THE WORLD.

SUGAR

SUGAR FOUND ITS WAY INTO ALMOST EVERY MEAL. SWEET OR NOT, SUGAR WAS PRESENT EVERYWHERE.

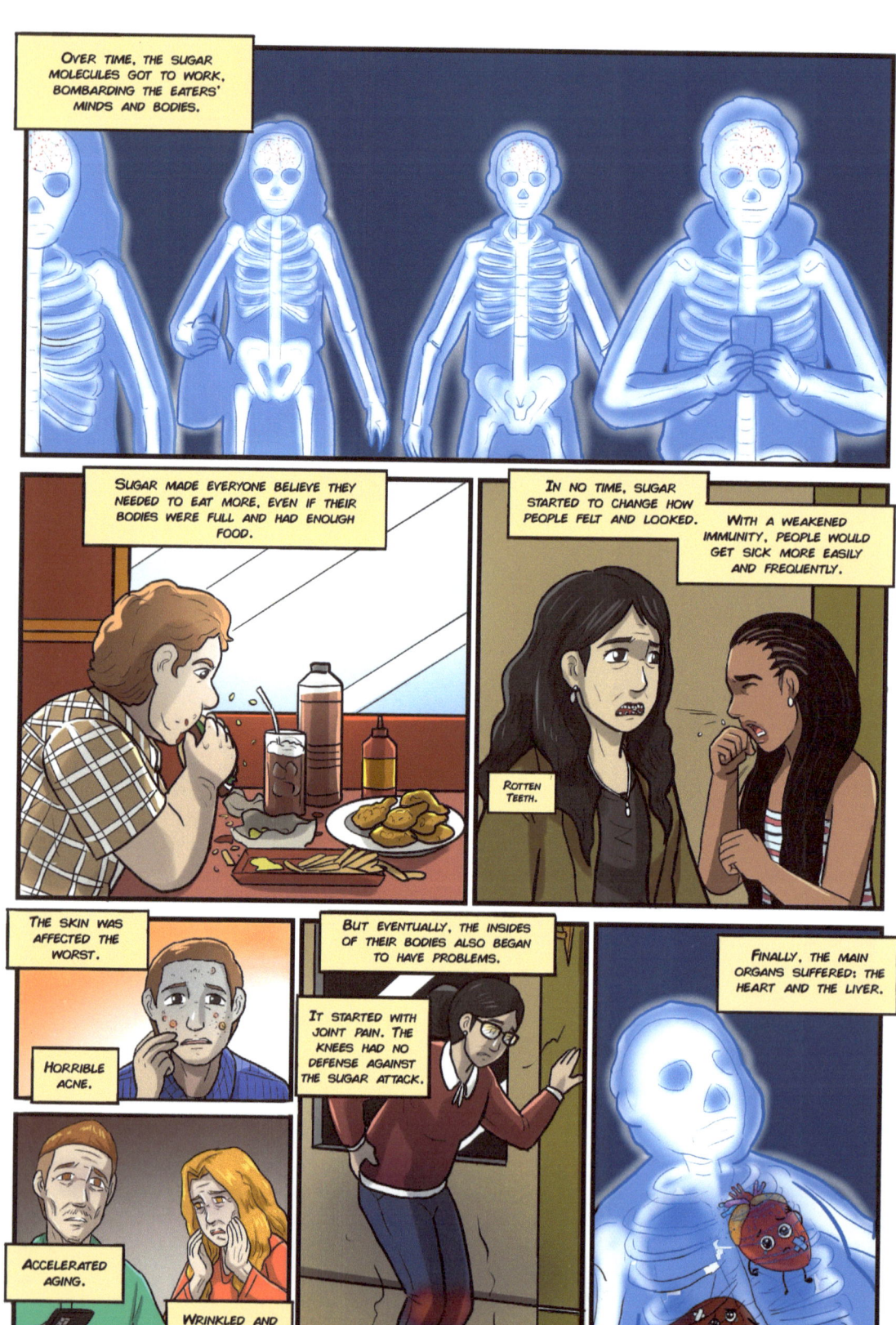

APPENDIX

TOO MUCH ADDED SUGAR IS NOT HEALTHY.

Children and teens should eat less than six teaspoons of added sugar daily. On average, American children eat sixteen teaspoons of added sugar per day. In one year, children eat over fifty-three pounds of sugar!

Look for zero added sugar on the food label.

COCA-COLA vs. TROPICANA'S APPLE CHERRY JUICE

Tropicana Apple Cherry Juice

Nutrition Facts

Serving Size:
8 fl oz

Amount Per Serving
Calories 140

	% Daily Value*
Total Fat 0g	0%
Sodium 0mg	0%
Total Carbohydrates 34g	12%
Dietary Fiber 4g	14%
Sugars 26g	
Includes 0g Added Sugars	0%
Protein 0g	
Vitamin D 0mcg	0%
Calcium 0mg	0%
Potassium 80mg	2%

* The % Daily Value (DV) tells you how much a nutrient in a serving of food contributes to a daily diet. 2000 calories a day is used for general nutrition advice.

INGREDIENTS: APPLE JUICE, BANANA PUREE AND CHERRY JUICE FROM CONCENTRATE (FILTERED WATER, APPLE JUICE, BANANA PUREE AND CHERRY JUICE CONCENTRATES), APPLE PUREE, CHICORY ROOT FIBER, NATURAL FLAVORS, FRUIT AND VEGETABLE JUICE CONCENTRATE (COLOR) AND ASCORBIC ACID (VITAMIN C).

Coca-Cola

Nutrition Facts

Serv. Size 1 Can

Amount Per Serving
Calories 140

	% Daily Value
Total Fat 0g	0%
Sodium 45mg	2%
Total Carb. 39g	14%
Total Sugars 39g	
Incl. 39g Added Sugars	78%
Protein 0g	

Not a significant source of sat. fat, *trans* fat, cholest., fiber, vit. D, calcium, iron and potas.

The Coca-Cola label has 39 grams of added sugar, and the Tropicana Apple Cherry Juice has 0 grams of added sugar.

Note: One teaspoon of sugar equals four grams of sugar.

What is added sugar?

Added sugar has been added to food by man.

Common foods with added sugar include sodas, sports drinks, fruit drinks, sweet tea, yogurts, ice cream, candy, cookies, cakes, pies, doughnuts, pastries, and cereals.

Added sugar is not in foods that come from the earth. Foods that come from the earth (or ground), like fruits and vegetables, do not have added sugar. They have natural sugar, which has important vitamins and minerals. For example, one banana has fifteen grams of sugar and zero grams of added sugar.

Healthier Options

1. Kite Hill Plain Unsweetened Yogurt – add frozen organic blueberries, an organic banana, and organic cinnamon raisin granola. For added sweetness, make a simple date paste by blending organic pitted dates with water, then add it to your yogurt.
2. Alter Eco No Added Sugar Cinnamon Raisin Organic Granola
3. Cascadian Farm No Added Sugar Vanilla Crisp Cereal
4. Magic Spoon Grain-Free Cereal Fruity Naturally Flavored
5. Simple Mills Organic All Purpose Baking Mix
6. Lakanto Sugar-free Maple Syrup
7. St. Joseph's Sugar-free Maple Syrup
8. Maple Grove Farms Sugar-free Maple Syrup
9. Rip Van Vanilla Wafer Cookies
10. So Delicious Vanilla Bean Coconut Ice-cream
11. Homemade oatmeal: Combine steel-cut oatmeal with apple, pear, and banana slices. Sprinkle with cinnamon and cook in an Instapot. No sugar needed!
12. Primal Kitchen's variety of sauces for dipping
13. Dr. Trina's drink: Mix ¼ a cup of your favorite 100% organic juice with ¾ cup of sparkling water.

Sugar Content in Drinks and Dips at Fast Food Restaurants

Burger King

Drinks:
OREO® Cookie Chocolate Shake 16 oz. – 93 gm or 23.25 tsp.
OREO® Cookie Shake 16 oz. – 88 gm or 22 tsp.
Hershey Chocolate Shake 16 oz. – 86 gm or 21.5 tsp.
Vanilla Shake 16 oz. – 81 gm or 20.25 tsp.
Coca-Cola® 20 oz. – 73 gm or 18.25 tsp.
Sprite® 20 oz. – 70 gm or 17.5 tsp.
Root Beer 20 oz. – 81 gm or 20.25 tsp.
Fanta® Orange 20 oz. – 77 gm or 19.25 tsp.
Hi-C® Fruit Punch 20 oz. – 75 gm or 18.75 tsp.
Minute Maid Lemonade 20 oz. – 67 gm or 16.75 tsp.

Dips:
Barbeque Sauce 1 Packet – 11 gm or 2.75 tsp.
Honey Mustard Sauce 1 Packet – 8 gm or 2 tsp.
Breakfast Syrup 1 Packet – 17 gm or 4.25 tsp.
Grape Jam 1 Packet – 6 gm or 1.5 tsp.
Strawberry Jam 1 Packet – 6 gm or 1.5 tsp.
Ketchup 1 Packet – 2 gm or 0.5 tsp.

Chick-fil-A

Drinks:
Cookies & Cream Milkshake 14.5 oz. – 84 gm or 21 tsp.
Chocolate Milkshake 14 oz. – 87 gm or or 21.75 tsp.
Strawberry Milkshake 14.5 oz. – 87 gm or 21.75 tsp.
Vanilla Milkshake 14.5 oz. – 80 gm or 20 tsp.
Sweetened Iced Tea 12 oz. – 31 gm or 7.75 tsp.

**The maximum amount of added sugar in a day
is six teaspoons or twenty-four grams.
One teaspoon of sugar equals four grams of sugar.**

Lemonade 14.5 oz. – 55 gm or 13.75 tsp.
Sun-Joy (½ Sweet Tea &; ½ Lemonade) 20 oz. – 43 gm or 10.75 tsp.
Coca-Cola® 12 oz. – 40 gm or 10 tsp.
Dr. Pepper® 15 oz. – 47 gm or 11.75 tsp.
Simply® Orange 11.5 oz. – 30 gm or 7.5 tsp.

Dips:
Barbeque Sauce 1 Packet – 9 gm or 2.25 tsp.
Honey Mustard Sauce 1 Packet – 10 gm or 2.5 tsp.
Polynesian Sauce 1 Packet – 13 gm or 3.25 tsp.
Sweet & Spicy Sriracha 1 Packet – 10 gm or 2.5 tsp.
Chick-fil-A® Sauce 1 Packet – 6 gm or 1.5 tsp.

Dairy Queen

Drinks:
Chocolate Shake 24 oz. – 128 gm or 32 tsp.
Carmel Shake 24 oz. – 124 gm or 31 tsp.
Hot Fudge Shake 24 oz. – 112 gm or 28 tsp.
Strawberry Shake 24 oz. – 105 gm or 26.25 tsp.
Vanilla Shake 24 oz. – 112 gm or 28 tsp.
Barq's Rootbeer Soda 21 oz. – 77 gm or 19.25 tsp.
Coca-Cola® 21 oz. – 68.25 gm or 17 tsp.
Sprite® 21 oz. – 67.10 gm or 16.78 tsp.

Dips:
Barbeque Dipping Sauce 1 cup – 16 gm or 4 tsp.
Honey Mustard Dipping Sauce 1 cup – 14 gm or 3.5 tsp.
Marzetti Dijon Honey 1 packet – 7 gm or 1.75 tsp.

**The maximum amount of added sugar in a day
is six teaspoons or twenty-four grams.
One teaspoon of sugar equals four grams of sugar.**

In-N-Out Burger

Drinks:
Chocolate Shake 15 oz. – 65 gm or 16.25 tsp.
Vanilla Shake 15 oz. – 50 gm or 12.5 tsp.
Strawberry Shake 15 oz – 100 gm or 25 tsp.
Coca-Cola® 22 oz. – 73 gm or 18.25 tsp.
7UP® 22 oz. – 64 gm or 16 tsp.
Root Beer 22 oz. – 81 gm or 20.25 tsp.
Pink Lemonade 22 oz. – 70 gm or 17.5 tsp.
Sweet Tea 19 oz. – 66 gm or 16.5 tsp.

Jack In The Box

Drinks:
Chocolate Shake with Whipped Topping 24 ounces (oz.) –128 grams (gm) per 32 teaspoons (tsp.)
Strawberry Shake with Whipped Topping 24 oz – 116 gm or 29 tsp.
OREO® Cookie with Whipped Topping 24 oz. – 105 gm or 26 tsp.
Vanilla Shake with Whipped Topping 24 oz. – 91 gm or 22.75 tsp.
Root Beer 20 oz. – 68 gm or 17 tsp.
Coca-Cola® 20 oz. – 62 gm or 15.5 tsp.
Fanta® Orange 20 oz. – 55 gm or 13.75 tsp.
Hi-C® Fruit Punch 20 oz. – 69 gm or 17.25 tsp.

Dips:
Barbeque Sauce 1 Packet – 9 gm or 2.25 tsp.
Honey Mustard Sauce 1 Packet – 9 gm or 2.25 tsp.
Teriyaki Sauce 1 Packet – 10 gm or 2.5 tsp.
Log Cabin Syrup 1 Packet – 18 gm or 4.5 tsp.
Grape Jelly 1 Packet – 9 gm or 2.25 tsp.
Strawberry Jam 1 Packet – 8 gm or 2 tsp.
Ketchup 1 Packet – 2 gm or ½ tsp.

**The maximum amount of added sugar in a day
is six teaspoons or twenty-four grams.
One teaspoon of sugar equals four grams of sugar.**

McDonald's

Drinks:
Mcflurry with M&M® Candies 12 oz. – 83 gm or 20.75 tsp.
Mcflurry with OREO® Cookies 12 oz. – 60 gm or 15 tsp.
Chocolate Shake 22 oz. – 106 gm or 26.5 tsp.
Vanilla Shake 22 oz. – 85 gm or 21.25 tsp.
Strawberry Shake – 22 oz. – 107 gm or 26.75 tsp.
Coca – Cola 21 oz. – 56 gm or 14 tsp.
Sprite® 21 oz. – 51 gm or 12.75 tsp.
Hi-C® Orange 21 oz. – 58 gm or 14.5 tsp.
Fanta® Orange 21 oz. – 55 gm or 13.75 tsp.
Sweet Tea 21 oz. – 29 gm or 7.25 tsp.
Lemonade 21 oz. – 54 gm or 13.5 tsp.

Dips:
Tangy Barbeque Sauce 1 Packet – 9 gm or 2.25 tsp.
Honey 1 Packet – 11 gm or 2.75 tsp.
Sweet and Sour Sauce 1 Packet – 10 gm or 2.5 tsp.
Hotcake Syrup 1 Packet – 33 gm or 8.25 tsp.
Grape Jam 1 Packet – 7 gm or 1.75 tsp.
Honey Mustard 1 Packet – 4 gm or 1 tsp.
Ketchup 1 Packet – 2 gm or 0.5 tsp.

**The maximum amount of added sugar in a day
is six teaspoons or twenty-four grams.
One teaspoon of sugar equals four grams of sugar.**

Red Robin

Drinks:
Monster 20 oz. Malt (Peaches & Cream) – 178 gm or 44.5 tsp.
Monster 20 oz. Milkshake (Peaches & Cream – 173 gm or 43.25 tsp.
Monster 20 oz. Malt (Chocolate) – 135 gm or 33.75 tsp.
Monster 20 oz. Milkshake (Chocolate) –128 gm or 32 tsp.
Monster 20 oz. Malt (Vanilla) – 127 gm or 31.75 tsp.
Monster 20 oz. Milkshake (Vanilla) – 119 gm or 29.75 tsp.
Orange Cream Soda 16 oz. – 65 gm or 16.25 tsp.
Lemonade with Peach Flavor 16 oz. – 75 gm or 18.75 tsp.
Fresh Brewed Sweet Tea (Peach) 16 oz. – 72 gm or 18 tsp.
Raspberry Cream Soda 16 oz. – 62 gm or 15.5 tsp.
Fresh Brewed Sweet Tea (Raspberry) 16 oz. – 60 gm or 15 tsp.

Dips:
Island Heat Sauce 1 packet – 29 gm or 7.25 tsp.
Smoke & Pepper Ketchup 1 packet – 17 gm or 4.25 tsp.
Whiskey River Bar Skew Sauce 1 packet – 28 gm or 7 tsp.
Sweet & Spicy Ketchup 1 packet – 30 gm or 7.5 tsp
Heinz 57 1 packet – 16 gm or 4 tsp.

Sonic

Drinks:
Hot Fudge Shake 20 oz. – 80 gm or 20 tsp.
Fresh Banana Shake 20 oz. – 70 gm or 17.5 tsp.
Chocolate Shake 20 oz. – 67 gm or 16.75 tsp
Carmel Shake 20 oz. – 67 gm or 16.75 tsp.
Strawberry Shake 20 oz. – 66 gm or 16.5 tsp.
OREO® Cheesecake Shake 20 oz. – 84 gm or 21 tsp.
Cheesecake Shake 20 oz. – 68 gm or 17 tsp.
OREO® Chocolate Shake 20 oz. – 84 gm or 21 tsp.

**The maximum amount of added sugar in a day
is six teaspoons or twenty-four grams.
One teaspoon of sugar equals four grams of sugar.**

OREO® Reese's Peanut Butter Master Shake 20 oz. – 75 gm or 19.5 tsp.

Barq's Rootbeer 20 oz. – 53 gm or 13.25 tsp.

Big Red 20 oz. – 45 gm or 11.25 tsp.

Coca-Cola 20 oz. – 48 gm or 12 tsp.

Dr. Pepper 20 oz. – 46 gm or 11.5 tsp.

Fanta Orange 20 oz. – 51 gm or 12.75 tsp.

Hi-C Fruit Punch 20 oz. – 50 gm or 12.5 tsp.

Mellow Yellow 20 oz. – 51 gm or 12.75 tsp.

Sun Drop 20 oz. – 48 gm or 12 tsp.

Sweet Ice Tea 20 oz. – 45 gm or 11.25 tsp.

Dips:

BBQ Sauce 1 packet – 7 gm or 1.75 tsp.

Signature Sauce 1 packet – 8 gm or 2 tsp.

Honey Mustard Sauce 1 packet – 4 gm or 1 tsp.

Country Gravy – 4 gm or 1 tsp.

Ketchup 1 packet – 2 gm or 1/2 tsp.

Steak 'n Shake

Drinks:

OREO® Red Velvet Milkshake 16 oz. – 130 gm or 32.5 tsp.

M&M's® Milkshake 16 oz. – 116 gm or 29 tsp.

Peppermint Chocolate Chip Milkshake 16 oz. – 115 gm or 28.75 tsp.

Birthday Cake Milkshake 16 oz. – 115 gm or 28.75 tsp.

Reese's® Peanut Butter Cup Milkshake 16 oz. – 111 gm or 27.75 tsp.

Barq's Rootbeer 22 oz. – 33 gm or 8.25 tsp.

Coke Classic 22 oz. – 30 gm or 7.5 tsp.

Minute Maid® Lemonade 22 oz. – 27 gm or 6.75 tsp.

Sprite® 22 oz. – 29 gm or 7.25 tsp.

Ice Tea Sweetened 20 oz. – 27 gm or 6.75 tsp.

(continued)

**The maximum amount of added sugar in a day
is six teaspoons or twenty-four grams.
One teaspoon of sugar equals four grams of sugar.**

Dips:
Frisco Sauce 1 packet – 8 gm or 2 tsp.
Barbecue Sauce 1 packet – 4 gm or 1 tsp.
Honey Mustard Sauce 1 packet – 8 gm or 2 tsp.
Ranch Dressing 1 packet – 1 gm or 0.25 tsp.

Wendy's

Strawberry Frosty 12 oz. – 47 gm or 11.75 tsp.
Chocolate Frosty 12 oz – 40 gm or 10 tsp.
Blueberry Pomegranate Lemonade 12 oz. – 58 gm or 14.5 tsp.
Pineapple Mango Lemonade 12 oz. – 63 gm or 15.75 tsp.
Strawberry Lemonade 12 oz. – 61 gm or 15.25 tsp.
Coca-Cola® 12 oz. – 48 gm or 12 tsp.
Sprite® 12 oz. – 44 gm or 11 tsp.
Root Beer 12 oz. – 48 gm or 12 tsp.
Fanta® Orange 12 oz. – 50 gm or 12 tsp.
Hi-C® Fruit Punch 12 oz. – 50 gm or 12.5 tsp.
Sweet Iced Tea 12 oz. – 66 gm or 16.5 tsp.

Barbecue Nugget Sauce 1 Packet – 4 gm or 1 tsp.
Honey Mustard Nugget Sauce 1 Packet – 3 gm or 0.75 tsp.
Sweet and Sour Nugget Sauce 1 Packet – 11 gm or 2.75 tsp.
S'Awesome Sauce 1 Packet – 3 gm or 0.75 tsp.
Ketchup 1 Packet – 2 gm or 0.5 tsp.

**The maximum amount of added sugar in a day
is six teaspoons or twenty-four grams.
One teaspoon of sugar equals four grams of sugar.**

Food Nutrition Sources

Barq's
https://www.barqs.com/products/root-beer

Burger King
https://bk-use1-prod.sites.rbictg.com/nutrition/nutrition.pdf

Chick-fil-A
https://www.chick-fil-a.com/nutrition-allergens

Coca-Cola
https://us.coca-cola.com/products/coca-cola/original

Dairy Queen
https://www.dairyqueen.com/en-us/nutrition/treats/

https://www.nutritionix.com/i/dairy-queen/marzetti-dijon-honey-mustard/
23cb31342295b85c6b17d425

In-N-Out Burger
https://www.in-n-out.com/menu/nutrition-info

Jack in the Box
http://assets.jackinthebox.com/pdf_attachment_settings/106/value/
Nutritional_Facts.pdf

static.jackinthebox.com/pdfs/nutritional_brochure.pdf

McDonald's
https://www.mcdonalds.com/us/en-us/about-our-food/nutrition-calculator.html

https://www.mcdonalds.com/us/en-us/product/grape-jam.html#accordion-
c921f9207b-item-842cb18782

https://www.mcdonalds.com/us/en-us/product/hotcake-syrup.html#accordion-
c921f9207b-item-842cb18782

Red Robin
https://www.redrobin.com/sites/default/files/2023-07/0623_NS_RRGB-DONT-ST%20%281%29.pdf

Sonic
https://online.sonicdrivein.com/nutrition/nutrition.pdf?v=03-01-2023

Sprite
https://www.sprite.com/products/sprite

Steak 'n Shake
https://cos-steak-n-shake.s3.us-west-2.amazonaws.com/production/wp-content/uploads/2023/03/03144417/Nutrition-Facts_03.03.23.pdf

http://static5.fitbit.com/foods/Barbecue+Sauce/39371

https://www.nutritionix.com/i/steak-n-shake/frisco-sauce/58ef23546ef9f2c1234850ff

https://www.nutritionix.com/i/steak-n-shake/honey-mustard-dressing/513fc996927da70408003dbe

Tropicana
https://www.nutritionix.com/i/tropicana-essentials/fiber-fruit-juice-drink-apple-cherry/5dfdc55bf33b25853aa368fd

Wendy's
https://order.wendys.com/categories?site=menu&lang=en_US

https://fastfoodnutrition.org/wendys/calculator

Nutrition facts in this book may vary depending on the source.

DR. TRINA WIGGINS is a board-certified pediatrician, fitness champion, first African American competitive gymnast for Stanford University, wellness advocate, and speaker. Visit her at www.opt2bfit.com and www.trinawiggins.com.

Connect and Share

If you enjoyed *The Sugar Attack* and believe it can help others, please share this book by purchasing copies for others, and be sure to leave a review on the website where you purchased it. Visit trinawiggins.com to connect with the author.

www.ingramcontent.com/pod-product-compliance
Lightning Source LLC
Chambersburg PA
CBHW041447120626
46547CB00002B/375